THE

ASSASSINATION

of

ABRAHAM LINCOLN

ROBERT E. JAKOUBEK

Spotlight on American History
The Millbrook Press • Brookfield, Connecticut

Cover photograph courtesy of the Library of Congress

Photographs courtesy of: the Library of Congress: pp. 6, 11, 26, 49,
53, 55; Granger: pp. 8, 23, 35, 41; Bettmann Archive: pp. 14,
19; Lloyd Ostendorf: pp. 25, 30; North Wind: p. 32; National
Portrait Gallery: pp. 43, 44; National Archives: p. 56

Library of Congress Cataloging-in-Publication Data
Jakoubek, Robert E.
The assassination of Abraham Lincoln / by Robert E. Jakoubek.
p.   cm.—(Spotlight on American history)
Includes bibliographical references and index.
Summary: Discusses the day Lincoln was shot and the weeks
following his assassination, including the manhunt for John Wilkes
Booth and his co-conspirators.
ISBN 1-56294-239-5
1. Lincoln, Abraham, 1809–1865—Assassination—Juvenile literature.
[1. Lincoln, Abraham, 1809–1865—Assassination.] I. Title. II. Series.
E457.5.J34 1992   973.7′092—dc20   92-10900 CIP AC

Published by The Millbrook Press
2 Old New Milford Road, Brookfield, Connecticut 06804

Contents

The Assassination of
ABRAHAM LINCOLN

Abraham Lincoln on April 9, 1865,
five days before his assassination.

MR. LINCOLN

On Good Friday, April 14, 1865, Abraham Lincoln, the president of the United States, arose just past seven and walked quietly from his bedroom on the second floor of the White House to the library, an oval-shaped room a few doors away.

He took a chair near the center of the room and, as he did every morning, read a chapter from the Bible. When he finished, the president got up and ambled down a private hallway that led from the library to his office.

He sat down at an upright mahogany desk where he looked over his mail, endorsed for deposit a check for five hundred dollars, and wrote out a few notes, one to Secretary of State William Henry Seward, another to his commanding general, Ulysses S. Grant.

It was by now nearly eight o'clock and the president hurried downstairs. There, in the family dining room, his wife Mary and his sons Tad and Robert were having breakfast.

*In 1861, four years before his death, Lincoln, his
wife Mary, and his sons Willie, Robert, and Tad gathered
in the White House dining room for a family portrait.*

"Good morning, Mr. Lincoln," his wife said as he took his
place at the table. To his right sat the Lincolns' youngest son,
twelve-year-old Tad. On most days Tad would have been the subject of his father's full and kind attention, but at breakfast this
morning it was Robert, age twenty-two, his eldest son, whom the
president was most glad to see. Robert had not been home for
several months, not since February when he had joined the army
and had gone off to war.

Seeing his son back at the breakfast table sent Lincoln's spirits soaring. Not only was the Lincoln family together once more, but before long, other American families would also be reunited. And so too would the United States be made one nation again. After four bloody years, the Civil War was nearly over. The Confederacy, the government of the rebellious southern states, had been defeated. Just five days before, Robert himself had witnessed the surrender of General Robert E. Lee and his Army of Northern Virginia at Appomattox Court House.

Robert had, in fact, brought a portrait of Lee with him to the breakfast table. The president examined it with interest. "It is a good face," he said. "It is the face of a noble, brave man. I am glad the war is over at last." Robert, who had been serving on the staff of General Grant, the Union commander, told his father all about the surrender.

The conversation of father and son was interrupted only when the president learned that the Speaker of the House was waiting to see him. The meeting started the president's official day. He was in a grand mood. His next visitor, John A. J. Creswell, a former senator from Maryland, recalled that Lincoln "grasped my hand with the enthusiasm of a schoolboy and repeated the exclamation, 'The war is over!' " But in a moment or two, Creswell said, "he stopped, grew serious and added: 'But it has been an *awful* war, Creswell, it has been an awful war!' "

He was like that all day. One moment the president would celebrate the end of hostilities, the next he would remember how costly victory had been. Over six hundred thousand soldiers, Union and Confederate, lay dead.

But a victory it had unquestionably been. Under Lincoln's leadership slavery had been destroyed. The South would be forced to end its dependence on slaves to cultivate cotton. And, not least of all, the war settled the question of whether a state could secede from the Union.

In mid-morning, almost out of habit, the president put on his tall beaverskin hat and left for the War Department. The White House did not have a telegraph. So, during the four years of war, at least twice a day, Lincoln had walked the short way to the War Department to receive the latest reports of the fighting. On this day, he was anxious to get the news from North Carolina, where a Confederate army was being hunted down by the Union forces of General William Tecumseh Sherman.

There was little news from the front. Lincoln dropped in to see Secretary of War Edwin M. Stanton, the civilian head of the army. Throughout the war, Stanton had worried that Lincoln might be kidnapped or assassinated by Confederate sympathizers. The city was crawling with them, he said, and Lincoln had too little protection.

No sooner had Lincoln sat down in Stanton's office than the secretary started in. He knew that the president and Mrs. Lincoln had invited General Grant and his wife Julia to attend the theater with them that evening. It was too dangerous, Stanton said.

Lincoln assured Stanton that he would have a guard with him at the theater. Since November 1864, he had been accompanied by a police bodyguard whenever he left the White House.

That was his only precaution. When Stanton tried to increase his guard, Lincoln overruled him. "It would never do," he said, "for a president to have guards with drawn sabers at his door, as if he fancied he were . . . an emperor." In a democracy, he said another time, it is important "that the people know I come among them without fear."

News from the front was brought daily to President Lincoln during the long years of the Civil War. Battles like this one at Gettysburg caused Lincoln much sadness. He was determined that "these dead shall not have died in vain."

By eleven o'clock, the president had returned to the White House. Upstairs in his office, he convened a meeting of his Cabinet. General Grant joined the secretaries of the various departments who sat around a slightly cramped rectangular table.

Lincoln startled everyone by telling them why he expected good news very soon. Last night he had had a dream. It was the same dream that had come to him before nearly every great Union victory.

Secretary of the Navy Gideon Welles asked him to describe it. It took place at sea, the president said: "I seemed to be in some indescribable vessel, moving with great rapidity toward an indefinite shore." General Sherman in North Carolina must be nearing victory, Lincoln insisted. "I know of no other very important event which is likely just now to occur," he said.

2

JOHN WILKES BOOTH

"There comes the handsomest man in Washington," said Henry Clay Ford when he saw the actor John Wilkes Booth striding toward him. It was slightly after twelve noon, Friday, April 14, and Ford, the treasurer of Ford's Theatre on Tenth Street in Washington, was at work in his office. He knew Booth well. The actor had appeared in a production at the theater two years before and ever since had been coming by to pick up his mail.

A month short of his twenty-seventh birthday, Booth looked every inch the leading man. His fine profile, hazel eyes, strong chin, thick, black hair, and athletic build were the envy of his fellow performers.

He had entered into a career on the stage as if it was the most natural thing in the world. And, in his family, it was. Booth's father had been a famed English actor. His older brother, Edwin, reigned as America's foremost classical performer, renowned for his portrayal of Hamlet.

*John Wilkes Booth,
the mastermind behind
the assassination plot,
was a flamboyant per-
former who, at the time
of Lincoln's murder,
was thought to be one
of the most promising
actors of the day.*

On that April afternoon, Booth noticed a little more activity and excitement than usual in Ford's office. A few hours before, a messenger from the White House had come by and picked up tickets for that evening's performance of *Our American Cousin*. It was all set, Ford told Booth. The president and Mrs. Lincoln would be accompanied by General and Mrs. Grant. They would be sitting in a special box that overlooked the stage. Ford joked that Jefferson Davis, the president of the Confederacy, and General Lee would be in another box—as prisoners.

That got a rise from Booth, as Ford surely knew it would. Booth passionately supported the Confederacy and seldom passed by a chance to denounce everything connected with the Union cause. As if on cue, he told Ford how bitterly he resented Lee's surrender at Appomattox.

Booth's love for the southern cause was extravagant. Even Edwin Booth concluded that his brother was insane on the subject.

Booth believed that slavery, the South's "peculiar institution," was a wonderful thing. "This country was formed for the *white*, not for the *black* man," he wrote. Slavery, he went on, was "one of the greatest blessings (both for themselves and us) that God had ever bestowed upon a favored nation."

Abraham Lincoln stood for all Booth detested. It was Lincoln who had been elected president by promising to halt the expansion of slavery; Lincoln who resolved not to let the southern states secede from the Union and form their own Confederate nation; Lincoln who was the commander-in-chief of the armies that were conquering the South. And, above all, it was Lincoln who on January 1, 1863, had issued the Emancipation Proclamation, freeing the slaves in the South. That had transformed the war to restore the Union into a war to end slavery.

There was no end to Booth's rage. A few nights before, on April 11, he and some friends had stood in a light mist on the White House lawn and listened to Lincoln deliver his first speech since Lee's surrender. The president spoke of the possibility that newly freed slaves in the South would be accorded the right to vote. It was too much for Booth. "Something decisive must be done," he confided in his diary.

FOR YEARS Booth had been doing his best to serve the Confederacy. He had done some spying and had passed his information on to other Confederate agents. He had bought medical supplies in the North and saw to it that they got to southern hospitals. But he wanted to do more. He wanted to do something grand and theatrical, something people would remember forever.

Booth dreamed up a vast, monstrous scheme. He would kidnap President Lincoln and take him off to Richmond, Virginia, the Confederate capital. There, he would turn the president over to the Confederate government, which could hold him for ransom. The president, Booth reasoned, could be exchanged for the Confederate prisoners of war then languishing in northern prison camps.

The plan was farfetched, but it appealed to some in the Confederate government. As their military position worsened by the day, Confederate leaders were willing to at least consider the desperate move of kidnapping Lincoln. Several Confederate agents encouraged Booth, whom they knew from his previous work for them, to proceed with his attempt on Lincoln.

Bolstered by this support, Booth went to work. First of all, he needed help. In the late summer of 1864, in a room at Barnum's

Hotel in Baltimore, he explained his idea to two old friends, Samuel B. Arnold and Michael O'Laughlin. Both were former Confederate soldiers, anxious to strike a blow at the Union.

Booth poured them drinks, offered them cigars, and explained how it could be done. As nearly everyone in Washington knew, during the stifling days of summer the Lincolns lived in a cottage on the grounds of the United States Soldier's Home, a federal facility just outside Washington. Located on a shady hill, the place offered some relief from the relentless heat of the capital. Every summer's day, Lincoln commuted the four miles (6.7 kilometers) to his White House office. Sometimes he rode alone on horseback. More often, he traveled by carriage. But nearly always his guard was light. A few well-prepared men, Booth said, could easily overpower the guards and abduct the president. Persuaded, Arnold and O'Laughlin swore their allegiance to Booth.

Seizing the president would be one thing. Getting him from Washington to Richmond would be quite another. Once more Booth would need help. He found it in the autumn of 1864, when he met John Harrison Surratt, a thirty-two-year-old courier for the Confederacy.

Surratt considered Booth's plot for kidnapping Lincoln breathtaking, and Booth valued his assistance. From his work as a secret dispatch rider for the Confederacy, Surratt knew well the backroads between Washington and Richmond. He could locate the best escape routes and keep the kidnappers a step ahead of any pursuers.

During the fall and winter of 1864–65, Booth and Surratt recruited others to the conspiracy. Surratt brought in George A. Atzerodt, a down-and-out carriage painter who kept a boat on the Potomac River. He had ferried Confederate spies across the river and promised to do the same for Booth. David E. Herold, who claimed he knew the escape routes out of Washington like the back of his hand, also signed on. The last to join the plot was Lewis Thornton Powell, who went by the name Lewis Paine. A powerfully built man with a violent temper, Paine had served in the Confederate army before deserting. He came to know and greatly admire Booth, called him "Captain," and said he would follow him anywhere.

A wealthy man from his stage career, Booth was able to lavishly finance the plot he had hatched. He paid the conspirators. He bought them weapons. He kept horses for them stabled in and around Washington, and, to lay plans, he visited Surratt at the boardinghouse Surratt's mother ran in Washington. The others, too, frequently showed up at Mrs. Surratt's house. By March of 1865, everything seemed to be falling into place.

Everything except for getting at the president. It would not be until June or July that Lincoln would be living at the Soldier's Home again—three long months before he would be a convenient target.

Booth could not wait. On March 15, 1865, he announced a change in plans. Around midnight, in a private dining room at Gautier's restaurant on Pennsylvania Avenue in Washington, he assembled his six fellow conspirators—Arnold, O'Laughlin, Surratt, Atzerodt, Herold, and Paine. While his friends enjoyed Booth's hospitality, they listened with amazement as he laid out a new plan. Lincoln, he said, loved going to the theater. They would wait for an evening when the president was in his box at Ford's Theatre, seize him while he was watching a play, handcuff him, lower him to the darkened stage, and then hurry him out the back door.

This reward poster, issued five days after Lincoln's death, shows the eight conspirators in the plot against Lincoln. Mrs. Surratt, in the center, was implicated only because the men used her house as a meeting place.

The six conspirators could not believe their ears. Booth wanted them to kidnap the president of the United States in front of a theater audience! Arnold spoke out most strongly. He gave Booth a week to come up with a more practical scheme.

Two days later, on March 17, Booth had a better idea. He had heard that the president would be attending the performance of a play at a military hospital that very afternoon. Booth sprang into action and rounded up his cohorts. The hospital was located on the same road as the Soldier's Home, and all their original ideas for abduction and escape could be used. Armed and ready, the conspirators rode to a tavern near the hospital. Booth rode off to find out when the play at the hospital would be finished.

In a little while, Booth rejoined his friends. He looked pale and angry. Lincoln had not gone to the hospital after all. For Arnold and O'Laughlin this fiasco was the last straw. They left Washington and had nothing else to do with the conspiracy. Surratt, too, began to have his doubts and decided to keep his distance from Booth.

As Booth was losing followers, the Confederacy was losing the war. On Sunday, April 2, 1865, facing certain defeat, President Jefferson Davis and most of the Confederate government fled Richmond. The capital quickly fell to Union troops and, on April 5, Lincoln himself toured the ruined city.

Booth now abandoned the kidnapping plot. He had no choice. Even if by some wild chance he and his dwindling band captured Lincoln, there was no longer any government in Richmond to whom the president could be delivered. But Booth refused to give up. In fact, he decided that he could single-handedly save the dying southern nation.

Depressed and drinking heavily, Booth got it into his head that if Lincoln and his government were eliminated there would be some sort of political revolution. Left leaderless at the moment of its victory, the North might yet be vanquished.

So it was that John Wilkes Booth decided to murder Abraham Lincoln. And, for good measure, he and his conspirators would kill General Grant, Vice President Andrew Johnson, Secretary of State William Henry Seward and, if they had time, Secretary of War Stanton.

When he found out in the office of Ford's Theatre at noon-time on April 14 that the president would definitely be coming to the theater that evening, Booth knew instantly his time had come.

3

"YOUR GREAT CHEERFULNESS"

By one-thirty the Cabinet meeting in the president's office was breaking up. Lincoln had led a long discussion about the reconstruction of the Union. On the subject of the defeated South, the president made his views clear. "I hope there will be no persecution, no bloody work, after the war is over," he said. "No one need expect me to take part in hanging or killing those men, even the worst of them."

Not advocating revenge did not mean Lincoln favored leniency toward the South. The southern states, he believed, must be made to extend certain basic rights of citizenship to the former slaves. At the Cabinet meeting, Lincoln seemed to be leaning toward using forceful persuasion to achieve that goal. He agreed to a proposal offered by Stanton to have a postwar military occupation of North Carolina and Virginia.

As the Cabinet members filed out of the room, General Grant lingered behind. He wanted to decline the Lincolns' invitation to the theater that evening. Grant expressed his regret to Lincoln, saying that he and Mrs. Grant would be leaving Washington shortly to join their children in New Jersey.

The president said he understood and did not press Grant very hard to reconsider. Perhaps he knew that the general was not being altogether candid. The family business could have easily waited a day. In truth, the general and his wife were declining because Julia Grant could not stand Mary Lincoln and wanted no part of an evening with her.

Lincoln presented the Emancipation Proclamation to his Cabinet on September 22, 1862. When it went into effect on January 1, 1863, slaves in the rebellious Southern states were declared free, but the slavery issue was far from dead.

After saying good-bye to Grant, the president went to his desk, where he signed papers and received visitors. At three o'clock he hurried downstairs to meet Mary. He had promised to accompany her on a carriage ride.

Outside, it had turned into a rather pleasant day. The coachman helped Mrs. Lincoln into the carriage, and the president slid into the back seat close to her. They rolled down the gravel driveway and out through the White House gates, and made their leisurely way in the direction of the Washington Navy Yard.

Mary Lincoln had seldom seen her husband in better spirits. "Dear Husband," she said, "you almost startle me by your great cheerfulness."

"And well I may feel so," he replied. "I consider this day, the war, has come to a close."

As they rode along Lincoln began to speak hopefully of the days to come: "We must *both* be more cheerful in the future—between the war and the loss of our darling Willie—we have both been very miserable."

"Our darling Willie" was the most painful topic Lincoln could bring up. In February 1862, Willie Lincoln, their eleven-year-old son, had died in the White House of a fever. Even three years later their grief was never far away.

But on this day Lincoln was looking ahead. He talked of what they should do after his term as president was up. They would, of course, go back to their home in Illinois. But he also wanted to travel. They would go to Europe, to California, maybe even to the place he had always dreamed of seeing—Jerusalem.

When they reached the Navy Yard along the Anacostia River, the president climbed down from the carriage to look at one of the ships. Around five, they were back at the White House.

Young Willie Lincoln, who died in the White House a year after his father became president.

Mary Todd Lincoln was never the same after her husband's death.
The remaining seventeen years of her life were spent in misery.

THE FIRST LADY

Abraham and Mary Todd Lincoln were married for twenty-three years. Like most marriages, theirs had its ups and downs, but neither could imagine life without the other. Once, at a White House reception, the president stood watching Mary entertaining guests. Smiling, he turned to a woman at his side. "My wife," he said with great feeling, "is as handsome as when she was a girl, and I, a poor nobody then, fell in love with her; and what is more, I have never fallen out."

Mary Lincoln's life after her husband's death was a tragedy. In 1871, her son Tad died of tuberculosis at the age of eighteen. After that, her mind gave way. She believed herself impoverished yet continued to spend lavishly on jewelry and clothing she never wore. In 1875, fearing "probable tragedy," her surviving son Robert brought insanity proceedings against her. A judge declared her "insane" and committed her to an asylum. The night after the trial she attempted suicide. After four months in the asylum, she was released and in 1876, after a second trial, declared sane.

Humiliated, the former first lady left the United States for a lengthy stay in France. In 1880, she returned to the care of relatives in Springfield. Nearly all of her time was spent in her lonely, candlelit bedroom, its windows closed, its curtains drawn. There she lay in bed, always to one side so as not to disturb "the president's place" next to her.

At 8:15 on the evening of July 15, 1882, she died.

At the dinner table with Tad and Robert, the president's good mood continued, but as he picked at his food he complained of being terribly tired. Nevertheless, the president thought seeing an amusing play would do him good. Mary sighed that she had a headache and would just as soon not go to the theater. When Lincoln said he did not want to go without her, she immediately changed her mind. Headache or not, the first lady would accompany her husband.

The Lincolns were a little late leaving the White House for the theater and were made later still by having to call for their guests. During the afternoon, after learning of the Grants' cancellation, Mary had asked along Major Henry J. Rathbone and his fiancée Clara Harris, the daughter of Senator Ira Harris of New York. Despite the last-minute nature of the invitation, they quickly accepted. After picking them up at the house of Senator Harris, the Lincolns and their young friends chatted lightheartedly while riding the six blocks to Ford's Theatre.

At the theater, the curtain was up and the play had begun. Many in the audience stirred restlessly, their eyes darting from the stage to the special box decorated with American flags and a picture of George Washington. They were expecting to see the president and General Grant. The president's plans to attend were well known, and Ford's management had raised its ticket prices for the occasion. But the box was empty and dark.

Suddenly, midway through the first act, there were noises from outside and signs of movement near the box. The actors on the stage stopped saying their lines and stood almost at attention. The audience rose and began to cheer. The orchestra leader sprang to his feet, lifted his baton, and the band blasted out "Hail to the Chief."

The president of the United States had arrived.

4

"MY GOD – THE PRESIDENT'S SHOT!"

As Abraham Lincoln was leaving the White House for Ford's Theatre, John Wilkes Booth was putting the final touches on his plans for committing murder. At eight o'clock, he gathered together his band of conspirators in a room at the Herndon House, a hotel a block away from Ford's Theatre. He had but three followers left, Lewis Paine, George Atzerodt, and David Herold. Surratt, O'Laughlin, and Arnold had all taken their leave.

Since discovering at noon that the president was definitely attending the theater, Booth had been a busy man. Throughout the afternoon, he had raced back and forth in Washington, alerting his cohorts, arranging for horses, attempting to secure escape routes, and setting things up for himself at Ford's Theatre. On one of his trips up and down Pennsylvania Avenue he had seen General and Mrs. Grant in a carriage. He learned from some bystanders that the Grants were going to New Jersey. Booth considered that he would have one less target at the theater.

Lewis Paine was ordered by Booth to kill Secretary of State William Seward as he lay in bed recovering from a carriage accident.

At the Herndon House, Booth laid out his plan. He himself would take care of Lincoln. Paine was to kill Secretary of State William Henry Seward. The secretary, they all agreed, was a sitting duck. Seward had been injured a few weeks before in a carriage accident and ever since had been bedridden in his house on Lafayette Square, just across from the White House. Paine readily accepted the assignment. Booth told Herold to wait until Paine was done, then to lead him out of the city.

Atzerodt was getting cold feet. Hearing that it was up to him to kill Vice President Andrew Johnson, Atzerodt said he had gotten into the affair for kidnapping, not murder. It was too late for second thoughts, Booth warned, but Atzerodt left the Herndon House unsure of what he was going to do.

Paine headed off toward Seward's house. Booth walked around the block to Ford's Theatre. He was there for only a few minutes, long enough to make sure that the president had arrived.

The play had resumed. In the spacious presidential box, Lincoln settled into a comfortable-looking rocking chair upholstered in black velvet. Mrs. Lincoln sat next to him, while Major Rathbone and Miss Harris took seats to the president's right. Within minutes, they were all caught up in the play.

Our American Cousin featured a time-worn plot: a backwoods American, mistaken for a rich man, is suddenly thrust into highly proper English society. The audience at Ford's that evening seemed to enjoy the performance enormously, frequently erupting into gales of laughter.

Perhaps it was a burst of laughter that convinced John F. Parker to go and see what was so funny. He got up from where he had been sitting and strolled around to a place where he had a good view of the stage. But Parker was not supposed to be watching the play. He was supposed to be protecting the president.

President Lincoln and his guests watched the play with no reason to suspect that Booth was lurking behind them, armed with a pistol and a knife.

Parker was an unlikely choice for a presidential bodyguard. A Washington, D.C., policeman, he had a record of tardiness, neglect of duty, and drunkenness. At one point, he had been almost fired from the force. Yet, somehow, he had been assigned to be one of Lincoln's police bodyguards.

With Parker's departure, the vestibule behind the presidential box was empty. Now, nearly anyone could walk right in.

The president laughed at the punch lines of *Our American Cousin* along with everyone else. Lincoln loved going to plays; he and Mary were the first president and first lady to attend the theater regularly.

While the president was enjoying the entertainment, Booth was slipping in and out of the theater. Some in the audience were glad to catch a glimpse of such a famous performer. No one suspected a thing. What could be more natural than seeing an actor in a theater?

Around nine o'clock, during the intermission that followed the first act, Booth dropped by the Star Saloon next door to the theater for a drink. From there he went to the stable behind Ford's and brought out his horse, a bay mare. At the back door of the theater he asked Edman Spangler, a scene shifter, to hold the horse until he returned for it. Busy moving scenery, Spangler passed the job on to "Peanut John" Burroughs, a boy who worked as a door-keeper for the theater.

The third act began. Lincoln, who had felt a little chill, got up and put on his long wool overcoat. It was a bit past ten o'clock. Booth left the theater one last time, again going to the Star Saloon.

In the president's box, Mary Lincoln moved closer to her husband. She placed her hand in his. "What will Miss Harris think of my hanging on to you so?" she asked softly.

"She won't think anything about it," Lincoln replied.

Booth reentered the theater and hurried up the winding stairs to the dress circle, or balcony seats. Armed with a small pistol and a dagger, he hummed a tune. He went to the door of the passage-way that led to the president's box. He paused and leaned against the wall. After a moment, he pushed open the door to the passage-way and stepped in. He closed the door behind him and barred it with a small piece of wood that he had placed in a corner earlier in the day. Now, no one could enter without forcing the door open.

As he turned and walked down the passageway, John Wilkes Booth was ten feet (three meters) from the president—from the man he hated more than any other in the world.

"Don't know the manner of good society, eh?" cried the actor playing the American cousin. "Wal, I guess I know enough to turn you inside out, old gal—you sockdolgizing old mantrap." The audience cackled with laughter.

Booth eased open the door to the president's box. Its four occupants were laughing, their eyes on the stage. The Lincolns were still holding hands. The president rocked back and forth slightly in his chair. Booth had in his right hand a .44 caliber derringer that contained one bullet. He lifted it to within six inches of the back of the president's head, and fired.

The shot was tremendously noisy, and smoke from the gun filled the air. The president had been leaning a little forward, looking at the audience in the orchestra seats below. When the bullet hit, his right arm jerked up. He slumped in his seat and did not move. Mary reached toward him.

Major Rathbone looked to his left and saw Booth standing amid the smoke. The major leaped toward him. Booth dropped his derringer and got the dagger in his right hand. He tried to strike at Rathbone's chest but stabbed him in the arm instead. The blow opened a deep gash, cutting the major nearly to the bone.

Booth sprang to the front of the box, next to where Mary was sitting. Rathbone followed, grabbing at him. "Stop that man!" the major yelled. Clara Harris, seeing what had happened, screamed "Won't somebody stop that man?" Booth seized the railing at the front edge of the box and, like a man swinging himself across a

Booth broke his leg when he jumped to the stage from Lincoln's box, but still managed to get out of the theater and escape on his waiting horse.

fence, jumped over. He meant to leap down the nine or ten feet (three meters) to the stage, but Rathbone got hold of his coat and upset his balance. One of his spurs caught in the decorations on the front of the box. Booth's athletic jump became an ungainly fall. He landed hard on his left foot and knee, so hard that a bone in the leg snapped. In excruciating pain, he struggled to his feet and limped across the stage.

As the audience sat in stunned disbelief, he brandished the dagger and shouted out, "Sic semper tyrannis," a Latin phrase meaning "Thus ever to tyrants." It was the motto of the Commonwealth of Virginia.

"My God—the president's shot!" shouted a man sitting in the dress circle opposite Lincoln's box. And then, everyone in the theater, all the nearly sixteen hundred people who seconds before had been laughing at an improbable comedy, heard the shrill screams of Mary Todd Lincoln. For a moment she stood and faced the theater. Then, she dropped to her knees next to the rocking chair. Her husband had not moved. Mary reached her arms around him and started weeping uncontrollably.

William Withers, the orchestra leader, was just then standing backstage near one of the exits trying to figure out, as he later said, "why they should fire off a pistol in *Our American Cousin*." Now he saw Booth limping toward him. "Let me pass!" Booth bellowed. "His eyes seemed starting from their sockets, and his hair stood on end. In his left hand there was a long dagger," Withers recounted. The orchestra leader stood his ground and Booth stabbed him in the neck. Withers fell, and Booth rushed out the door leading to the alley. He slugged and kicked "Peanut John" Burroughs, the boy holding his horse, mounted the steed, and galloped off down the alley.

*A*T THE SAME TIME, Lewis Paine was also trying to get away from Washington in a hurry. At around ten-fifteen, just as Booth was closing in on the president's box, Paine had knocked on the door of Secretary of State Seward's house. He said he had some medicine to deliver to the secretary. When Seward's son Frederick tried to question him further, Paine forced his way in, over-

*This woodcut shows Lewis Paine attacking the secretary of state.
Seward's young daughter Fanny could do nothing to stop him.*

powered young Seward, and knocked him out with the butt and barrel of his revolver.

He raced upstairs to the third floor. Clubbing Frederick had broken his gun, so as Paine burst into Seward's bedroom he drew his Bowie knife. Fortunately, the secretary was wearing a heavy metal brace on his neck. It was there to help heal his jaw, which had been injured in the carriage accident. The brace partly protected him from Powell's knife, saving his life. All the same, Paine managed to land three blows before Seward could roll himself out of bed and onto the floor.

A nurse and Seward's other son, Augustus, flew into the room and wrestled Paine away. Shouting "I'm mad, I'm mad," Paine ran downstairs and out of the house.

Outside, David Herold had been waiting for Paine, ready to lead him out of town. But the sounds of struggle coming from the house had frightened him. He ran off looking for Booth.

George Atzerodt just ran off. Instead of killing Vice President Johnson, he spent the evening drifting from one saloon to another. Having drunk away whatever remained of his courage, he disappeared into Maryland.

5

"NOW HE BELONGS
TO THE AGES"

Ford's Theatre was in a complete uproar. In the president's box, Mary Lincoln continued to clutch her husband's motionless body. Major Rathbone rushed from the box and into the passageway looking for help. There he removed the piece of wood Booth had used to bar the door. The door slammed open and two men, both doctors, dashed in.

Dr. Charles A. Leale reached the box first and at once bent over to examine the unconscious president. With the help of some of the others now pouring in to the box, he lifted Lincoln from his chair and laid him on the floor. Probing about, Leale located the wound at the rear of Lincoln's head. He removed a blood clot and saw where the bullet had smashed into his brain.

Right then, Leale knew the president was going to die.

On the floor, Lincoln stopped breathing and Leale could not find a pulse. He applied artificial respiration and the president started breathing again. Leale stood up and said, "His wound is mortal; it is impossible for him to recover."

The box was now filled with people. Clara Harris led Mary Lincoln to a sofa and tried to comfort her. Doctors and ranking military officers who had been in the audience pushed their way in. Some suggested returning the president to the White House. The doctors advised against it and insisted he be moved to someplace nearby.

They settled on the house directly across Tenth Street from the theater. There the president could be placed in a bed and ministered to properly. Using a makeshift stretcher, the doctors and several soldiers carried Lincoln, head first, out of the theater and across the street to the three-story house, which belonged to William Petersen, a local tailor. Major Rathbone, dripping blood from his arm the whole way, escorted Mrs. Lincoln.

Inside Petersen's house, the president was carried to a walnut four-poster bed in a room at the rear of the first floor. The room belonged to William T. Clark, a War Department clerk who boarded with Petersen. The bed was not long enough for Lincoln's tall body, and the doctors had to stretch the unconscious president out diagonally.

Seeing him motionless on the cramped bed, Mary rushed to his side and fell to her knees. She cried his name and begged him to reply. Gently, the doctors asked her to leave the room so they could examine her husband thoroughly. She was led across the hall to a parlor at the front of the house. "I cannot recall a more pitiful picture than that of poor Mrs. Lincoln, almost insane with sudden agony, moaning and sobbing out that terrible night," said a general who was in the house.

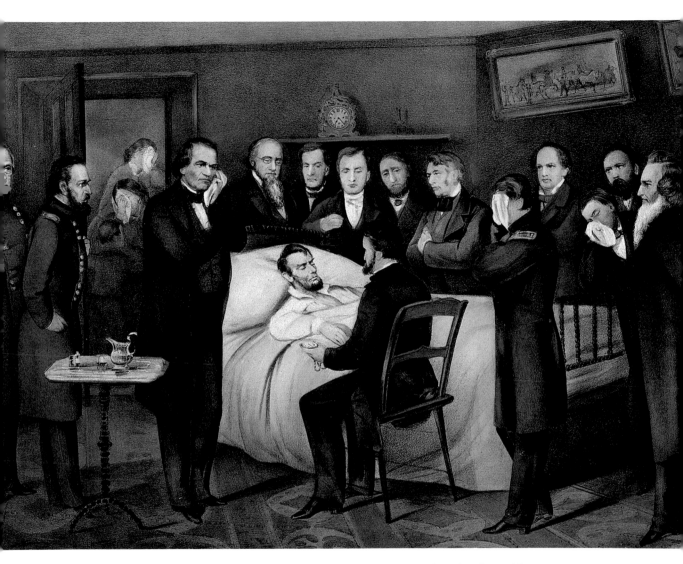

Those who cared for Lincoln spent a night of grief and pain at his bedside, hoping that by some miracle the president would survive.

By eleven o'clock, word of the shooting had spread throughout Washington. Crowds that had earlier been celebrating the end of the war now surged through the streets in a state of near panic. Wild rumors were told and retold. Not only had the president been assassinated, said one, but so had the secretary of state, all of the Cabinet, and General Grant.

Secretary of War Edwin Stanton got to the Petersen house shortly after eleven o'clock and promptly took charge. Setting up headquarters in the room next to where the president lay, Stanton started barking out orders. He sent an armed guard for Vice President Johnson and ordered all military forces around Washington to be placed on alert.

Shortly, Stanton ordered an aide to begin questioning witnesses from the theater. It did not take very long for them to identify the assassin as the actor John Wilkes Booth. By three in the morning, Stanton had passed his name to the newspapers and ordered his arrest.

The room where Lincoln lay was not large, measuring nine by seventeen feet (three by five meters). As the hours passed, it seemed to grow even smaller as doctors, congressmen, Cabinet members, and military officers hovered about the dying president. Robert Lincoln had arrived from the White House around eleven. Ushered in to the bedroom, he saw his father's lifeless form and swollen face. Young Lincoln broke down. It could not be true.

"I will go in!" said Charles Sumner at the doorway to the bedroom. Sumner, the tall, overbearing senator from Massachusetts, had had his share of political disagreements with the president. All that was forgotten now. Sumner took Lincoln's hand in his own and began talking to him. "It's no use, Mr. Sumner—he can't hear you," said one of the physicians. "He's dead."

Secretary of War Edwin Stanton took charge as it became clear that the president was dying. The vice president was sent for, and roadblocks were set up around the capital.

*With strong ties to the South, Andrew Johnson angered Congress
by issuing a general amnesty proclamation making Southern readmission
to the Union fairly painless for most states.*

THE NEW PRESIDENT

When the English novelist Charles Dickens met Andrew Johnson, he found his face to be "remarkable . . . indicating courage, watchfulness, and certainly strength of purpose." Coming from a humble background Johnson had risen to become a U.S. senator from Tennessee. When Tennessee seceded in 1861, Johnson remained loyal. He pledged "my blood, my existence" to save the Union. Wanting a loyal southerner on the ticket when he ran for reelection in 1864, Lincoln selected Johnson to be his running mate.

The new vice president got off on the wrong foot. At his inauguration on March 4, 1865, Johnson appeared to have had a little too much to drink and, when it came time for him to speak, made almost no sense.

Succeeding as president after Lincoln's assassination, Johnson proved to be altogether wrong for the job. He had little of Lincoln's enlightened vision and none of his political skills. By 1866, Johnson and the Republican leaders of Congress had fallen into a terrible wrangle over the reconstruction of the Union. The president favored leniency toward the defeated South and demanded little in the way of civil rights for the former slaves. Most Republicans in Congress favored just the opposite policy. Matters finally came to a head in 1868, when Congress attempted to impeach, or remove from office, President Johnson. By the smallest of margins—one vote in the Senate—Johnson retained the office of president.

"No, he isn't dead," Sumner said. "Look at his face; he is breathing." The senator bowed his head until it almost touched the president's pillow and started to cry.

By seven o'clock, Lincoln's pulse was weakening. Mary came to him a final time. At the bedside she fainted. After the doctors revived her she sat down beside her husband and kissed his face. "Love," she sobbed, "live but one moment to speak to me once—to speak to our children!"

Outside it had begun to rain. The steady downpour hammered at the windows of the Petersen house and soaked the crowd of onlookers in the street. The president could not hold out much longer. The men in the house gathered around the bed and watched silently as life ebbed away.

At 7:22 A.M. the noble heart of Abraham Lincoln stopped beating. A Presbyterian minister uttered a short prayer. "Now he belongs to the ages," murmured Stanton, tears flowing down his cheeks.

Robert guided his mother out of the Petersen house. As Mary stepped onto Tenth Street she glanced across to Ford's Theatre. "That dreadful house," she said. "That dreadful house." She would never set foot in a theater again.

At the White House, Robert saw to it that the first lady was put to bed. She could not sleep and tossed about furiously. Tad came to be with his mother. "Don't cry so, Mamma!" he begged, "don't cry, or you will make me cry, too! You will break my heart."

THE SADDEST DAYS

At the Navy Yard Bridge, which crossed the Anacostia River and led travelers out of Washington and into Maryland, Sergeant Silas T. Cobb figured it was about 10:30 P.M. Even though the war was nearly over, security precautions were still in place. After nine o'clock at night it was up to Cobb or one of the other guards to stop and question every person wishing to cross the bridge.

From the Washington side, a rider wearing a black suit and a black hat approached. He was spurring his horse to its top speed. Seeing the sentry, he slowed and stopped.

"Who are you, sir?" Cobb inquired.

"My name is Booth," the rider replied with remarkable candor, considering the circumstances.

"Where are you from?"

"The city."

"Where are you going?"

"I'm going home."

The exchange continued for several minutes, but Cobb heard nothing to arouse his suspicions. "I thought he was a proper person to pass—and I passed him," he said.

Ten minutes later, another lone horseman galloped up to the bridge. Once more Cobb questioned him. The man said his name was Smith and that he too was going home. The sergeant let him cross the bridge.

The second rider had been less truthful than the first. "Smith" was in fact David Herold. He had been on the run ever since leaving Seward's house and was now rushing to join up with Booth.

Somewhere along the road in Maryland, Herold caught up with Booth, and together the two men rode on to Surrattsville, a little hamlet not far from the Potomac River where John Surratt's mother, Mary, owned a tavern. Although she had moved to Washington and had rented the tavern to a man named John Lloyd, the conspirators still used the building as a refuge. Sometime in March, Surratt, Herold, and Atzerodt had come to the place and hidden two Spencer carbines and a box of ammunition.

Around midnight Booth and Herold reached the tavern. A drunken and confused John Lloyd let them take a carbine and a package containing a pair of field glasses. Booth did not dismount, and Herold brought him a drink of whiskey.

It would take more than whiskey to relieve the pain of a broken leg. Booth had to find a doctor. He knew where to go. In late 1864, on one of his trips to southern Maryland, Booth had met Dr. Samuel A. Mudd. Mudd had nothing to do with the conspiracy, but the doctor was a Confederate sympathizer and, at the moment, he was Booth's best hope for medical attention.

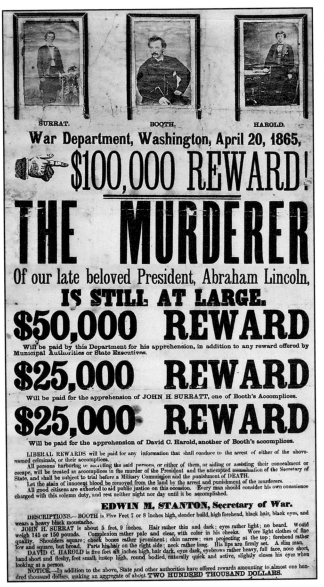

SURRAT.　　　BOOTH.　　　HAROLD.

War Department, Washington, April 20, 1865,

$100,000 REWARD!

THE MURDERER

Of our late beloved President, Abraham Lincoln,

IS STILL AT LARGE.

$50,000 REWARD

Will be paid by this Department for his apprehension, in addition to any reward offered by Municipal Authorities or State Executives.

$25,000 REWARD

Will be paid for the apprehension of JOHN H. SURRATT, one of Booth's Accomplices.

$25,000 REWARD

Will be paid for the apprehension of David C. Harold, another of Booth's accomplices.

LIBERAL REWARDS will be paid for any information that shall conduce to the arrest of either of the above-named criminals, or their accomplices.

All persons harboring or secreting the said persons, or either of them, or aiding or assisting their concealment or escape, will be treated as accomplices in the murder of the President and the attempted assassination of the Secretary of State, and shall be subject to trial before a Military Commission and the punishment of DEATH.

Let the stain of innocent blood be removed from the land by the arrest and punishment of the murderers.

All good citizens are exhorted to aid public justice on this occasion. Every man should consider his own conscience charged with this solemn duty, and rest neither night nor day until it be accomplished.

EDWIN M. STANTON, Secretary of War.

DESCRIPTIONS.—BOOTH is Five Feet 7 or 8 inches high, slender build, high forehead, black hair, black eyes, and wears a heavy black moustache.

JOHN H. SURRAT is about 5 feet, 9 inches. Hair rather thin and dark; eyes rather light; no beard. Would weigh 145 or 150 pounds. Complexion rather pale and clear, with color in his cheeks. Wore light clothes of fine quality. Shoulders square; cheek bones rather prominent; chin narrow; ears projecting at the top; forehead rather low and square, but broad. Parts his hair on the right side; neck rather long. His lips are firmly set. A slim man.

DAVID C. HAROLD is five feet six inches high, hair dark, eyes dark, eyebrows rather heavy, full face, nose short, hand short and fleshy, feet small, instep high, round bodied, naturally quick and active, slightly closes his eyes when looking at a person.

NOTICE.—In addition to the above, State and other authorities have offered rewards amounting to almost one hundred thousand dollars, making an aggregate of about TWO HUNDRED THOUSAND DOLLARS.

By April 20th, six days after the attacks, three of the conspirators remained at large.

Booth and Herold got to Dr. Mudd's at four o'clock in the morning. Booth had put on a false beard, and to his dying day Mudd would insist that he did not recognize Booth as being the man with the broken leg. The doctor dressed the leg, placed it in a splint, and let Booth and Herold have an upstairs bedroom for what was left of the night.

Leaving Mudd's late Saturday afternoon, April 15, Booth and Herold headed for the farm of Samuel Cox, a wealthy Confederate sympathizer. When they arrived early Sunday morning, Cox summoned his foster brother, Thomas A. Jones, and asked him to take care of the two weary men.

Jones knew exactly who Booth was and what he had done. But as a loyal Confederate he did what Cox asked. For the next six days Jones looked after Booth and Herold in their hiding place, a grove of pine trees near Port Tobacco, Maryland. He brought them food and the latest newspapers. Booth did not wish to miss a word of what was being written about himself and his deed. His plan was to lay low until it was safe to cross the Potomac, and then go more deeply into the South. Never, he told Jones, would they capture him alive.

SECRETARY OF WAR STANTON stayed in charge of the search for the president's assassin. Working tirelessly, Stanton assigned to the case everyone and everything he could think of. Police and detectives combed Washington. Cavalry regiments scoured southern Maryland.

Facing the full force of the federal government, Booth's motley group of conspirators soon cracked. On Monday, April 17, Michael O'Laughlin and Samuel Arnold, both part of Booth's original group of conspirators, were picked up. On the evening of the same day, officers swooped down on the Washington boardinghouse of Mary Surratt, the place on H Street frequented by Booth, Surratt, Powell, and Atzerodt. They arrested everyone in the house, but John Surratt was not among them. On April 14, he had been in upstate New York, on his way to Canada. Hearing of the assassination, he kept right on going, trying to get as far from Washington as he could. Eventually he reached Europe.

The authorities did have one stroke of luck at the Surratt place. While they were there, a burly man carrying a pickax appeared at the back door. He said he was there to dig a sewer for Mrs. Surratt. It seemed a little odd that he should be coming to work in the middle of the night, so the police arrested him along with the others. Only later did they learn he was Lewis Thornton Powell, alias Lewis Paine, the assailant of Secretary Seward.

On Thursday, April 20, pathetic George Atzerodt was tracked to the house of his cousin in Germantown, Maryland. An army sergeant found him moping around, depressed at having lost a girlfriend. Booth and Herold stayed at large, but Stanton's forces were closing in.

MEANWHILE, the grief-stricken nation began its long farewell to Abraham Lincoln.

On Monday evening, April 17, Lincoln's remains were brought to the East Room of the White House, where a large canopied platform had been constructed to hold the president's coffin. The following morning at nine-thirty, the White House gates swung open and the public began filing in to the hushed room and past the open coffin where Lincoln's head lay on a white pillow. The line of mourners stretched out for over a mile; people stood silently six and seven abreast.

At noon, the next day, Wednesday, April 19, the new president of the United States, Andrew Johnson, strode in to the East Room. With his arrival the funeral services for President Lincoln began. The room overflowed with more than six hundred people. Robert Lincoln stood at the foot of the coffin. He was the sole member of the family there; his mother was too distraught to come. General Grant sat alone near Lincoln's head. During the terrible battles of the war, Grant's face had seldom showed the slightest expression. Now, at the sight of the fallen president, he openly wept. He would later say that it was the saddest day of his life.

In the afternoon, Lincoln's body was borne up Pennsylvania Avenue to the Capitol. The hearse was followed by a riderless horse. It was Lincoln's favorite horse and, symbolizing its departed master, its stirrups faced backward. Thousands of troops marched behind. Everywhere there was the sound of muffled drums.

For a day, Lincoln lay in state under the great dome of the Capitol. Two lines of mourners, one on either side of the coffin and stretching out as far as anyone could see, slowly moved by.

On April 21, a special train, its nine cars painted black, steamed out of Washington carrying Lincoln's body. Church bells tolled mournfully as the train began its journey of nearly 1,700 miles (2,840 kilometers) to the prairies of Illinois.

A captive of grief, Mary Lincoln remained secluded at the White House. She had, however, rejected suggestions that Lincoln be buried in Washington. His home was in Illinois, she said, in Springfield. She also requested that the body of their son Willie be removed from its grave in Washington and taken on the train to Springfield. Father and son belonged together.

On April 19, 1865, Lincoln's funeral procession made its way up Pennsylvania Avenue to the Capitol, where his body was laid in state.

*T*HE GOVERNMENT had posted a one hundred thousand dollar reward for Booth's capture. Even such an enormous sum of money did not tempt Thomas Jones; he kept Booth's hiding place in the pine grove a secret. But the federal cavalry was everywhere in southern Maryland, and they were bound to come across him before long. On April 21, when the cavalry was off pursuing a false sighting of the assassin, Jones told Booth and Herold it was a good time to move on.

He guided them to the Potomac River, provided them with a boat, and watched them shove off for the Virginia shore. The strong current of the river prevented them from making it to Virginia until the next day. Finally across, the two men moved from the farm of one Confederate sympathizer to another.

On Monday afternoon, April 24, they came to the place of Richard H. Garrett, three miles (five kilometers) from Port Royal, Virginia. That night Garrett's eleven-year-old son shared his bedroom with Booth. He would always remember the visitor from Washington. "I had never seen such a face before," he recalled years afterward. "Jet black curls clustered about a brow as white as marble, and a heavy dark mustache shaded a mouth as beautiful as a babe's."

Planning to move on the next morning and wanting to get an early start, Booth and Herold spent the next night in a shed Garrett used for curing tobacco. Several hours before dawn a detachment of twenty-six soldiers, tipped off to Booth's whereabouts, swept onto the Garrett farm and surrounded the tobacco house. Herold ran out, waving his hands and shouting his innocence. When Booth did not follow, the lieutenant in command ordered that the building be set afire.

The flames gave the soldiers a good look at Booth. He stood with a crutch under each arm. The carbine was propped on his hip

[54]

Soldiers set fire to the barn where John Wilkes Booth was hiding to force him to surrender. In the end, however, a sergeant ended the life of Lincoln's assassin with one shot to the back of his head.

and he held a revolver in his hand. Stanton had issued orders that Booth be taken alive. Sergeant Boston Corbett disobeyed. An intensely religious man, Corbett would later say, "Providence directed me." His single shot struck Booth in the head. Two and a half hours later he died.

In Booth's pocket the soldiers discovered a diary. "I have too great a soul to die like a criminal," read one of his final entries.

Herold was taken back to Washington, where in May and June of 1865 he and the other conspirators were tried by a special military commission. All were convicted. Herold, Atzerodt, and Paine

*The public execution of four of the conspirators drew crowds
of mourners who felt that justice had been done.*

were sentenced to death. Mary Surratt, who had kept the rooming house where the plot was partly hatched, also received a death sentence. Arnold and O'Laughlin faced life imprisonment, as did the hapless Dr. Mudd. And Edman Spangler, the scene changer at Ford's Theatre who had arranged for someone to hold Booth's horse, was given six years at hard labor.

O<small>N THE DAY</small> the assassin was caught and killed, Lincoln's funeral train left Albany, New York, and rolled on toward Buffalo. As it had since leaving Washington, the train traveled at less than five miles (eight kilometers) an hour, allowing people along the tracks to gather and mourn as it passed. The procession across the country was the focus of an overwhelming outpouring of grief. In the towns where the train stopped, there were funeral corteges. In New York City, eighty-five thousand people marched behind the hearse carrying the coffin. Church bells tolled, and in the streets people wept.

In Cleveland, one hundred and fifty thousand came to an outdoor viewing of the body. In Indiana, bonfires burned by the tracks as the train slowly made its way westward.

On May 3, the train reached Springfield. After thirteen days and 1,662 miles (2,775 kilometers), it was only one hour late. "To this place, and the kindness of these people, I owe every thing," Lincoln had said on leaving Springfield for Washington and the White House in 1861. "Here I have lived a quarter of a century, and have passed from a young to an old man." And it was there, in Springfield, on May 4, 1865, that Abraham Lincoln and his son Willie were buried.

Chronology

1860	Abraham Lincoln is elected president of the United States.
February, 1862	Lincoln's son Willie dies at the White House at the age of 11; he is buried near Rock Creek in Washington, D.C.
January 1, 1863	Lincoln issues the Emancipation Proclamation.
Summer, 1864	John Wilkes Booth hatches a plot to kidnap Lincoln; he conspires with Samuel B. Arnold, Michael O'Laughlin, John Harrison Surratt.
Fall-Winter, 1864–65	Booth recruits George A. Atzerodt, Lewis Paine, and David E. Herold.
April 2, 1865	The Confederate capital of Richmond falls to Union troops.

April 9, 1865	Confederate general Robert E. Lee surrenders at Appomattox.
April 12(?), 1865	Booth abandons the kidnapping plan; he decides to murder Lincoln, General Grant, Vice President Andrew Johnson, Secretary of State William Henry Seward, and Secretary of War Edwin M. Stanton.
April 14, 1865	Lincoln is shot by John Wilkes Booth while attending a performance at Ford's Theatre.
April 15, 1865	Lincoln dies from the gunshot wound to his head.
April 17, 1865	Michael O'Laughlin, Samuel Arnold, and Lewis Paine are arrested at Surratt's boardinghouse.
April 19, 1865	Lincoln's funeral procession and services are held in Washington, D.C.
April 20, 1865	George Atzerodt is arrested in Germantown, Maryland.
April 21, 1865	A train leaves Washington, D.C., for Springfield, Illinois, carrying the bodies of Lincoln and his son Willie.
April 25, 1865	David Herold surrenders in Virginia; John Wilkes Booth is shot and killed.
May 4, 1865	Abraham Lincoln and his son Willie are buried in Springfield, Illinois.

Further Reading

Anderson, LaVere. *Mary Todd Lincoln: President's Wife.* New York: Chelsea House, 1991.

Bains, Rae. *Abraham Lincoln.* Mahwah, N.J.: Troll Associates, 1985.

D'Aulaire, Ingri, and Edgar P. Parin. *Abraham Lincoln.* New York: Doubleday, 1987.

Hargrove, Jim. *Abraham Lincoln: Sixteenth President of the United States.* Chicago: Children's Press, 1988.

Hayman, Leroy. *The Death of Lincoln: A Picture History of the Assassination.* New York: Scholastic, Inc., 1987.

Jacobs, William J. *Lincoln.* New York: Macmillan, 1991.

Kent, Zachary. *The Story of Ford's Theatre and the Death of Lincoln.* Chicago: Children's Press, 1987.

Bibliography

Direct quotations found throughout this book
appear in standard accounts of the times.

Bishop, Jim. *The Day Lincoln Was Shot*. New York: Harper and Brothers, 1955.

Bryan, George S. *The Great American Myth*. New York: Carrick and Evans, 1940.

Current, Richard. *The Lincoln Nobody Knows*. New York: Alfred A. Knopf, 1958.

Donald, David. *Charles Sumner and the Rights of Man*. New York: Alfred A. Knopf, 1970.

Hanchett, William. *The Lincoln Murder Conspiracies*. Urbana, Ill.: University of Illinois Press, 1983.

Kimmel, Stanley P. *The Mad Booths of Maryland.* Indianapolis: Bobbs-Merrill, 1940.

Kundhardt, Dorothy Meserve, and Philip B. Kundhardt, Jr. *Twenty Days.* New York: Harper and Row, 1965.

Luthin, Reinhard. *The Real Abraham Lincoln.* Englewood Cliffs, N.J.: Prentice-Hall, 1960.

Neely, Mark E., Jr. *The Abraham Lincoln Encyclopedia.* New York: McGraw-Hill, 1982.

Oates, Stephen B. *With Malice Toward None: The Life of Abraham Lincoln.* New York: Harper and Row, 1977.

Reck, W. Emerson, *A. Lincoln: His Last 24 Hours.* Jefferson, N.C.: McFarland, 1987.

Thomas, Benjamin. *Abraham Lincoln.* New York: Alfred A. Knopf, 1952.

———— and Harold M. Hyman. *Stanton: The Life and Times of Lincoln's Secretary of War.* New York: Alfred A. Knopf, 1962.

Tidwell, William A., with James O. Hall and David Gaddy Winfred. *Come Retribution: The Confederate Secret Service and the Assassination of Abraham Lincoln.* Jackson, Miss.: University Press of Mississippi, 1988.

Turner, Justin G. and Linda Levitt Turner. *Mary Todd Lincoln: Her Life and Letters.* New York: Alfred A. Knopf, 1972.

Weichmann, Louis J. *A True History of the Assassination of Abraham Lincoln and of the Conspiracy of 1865.* ed. by Floyd E. Risvold. New York: Alfred A. Knopf, 1975.

Index